Poetry Quarterly Magazine
—Summer 2010

©2010 Poetry Quarterly
Edited by Glenn Lyvers
Printed in the U.S.A.

Published By:
Poetry Quarterly Press
www.PoetryQuarterly.org
Mishawaka, IN

Poetry Quarterly is a not-for-profit Literary Magazine

Poetry Quarterly

Summer 2010

Contents

The Shadows	Patrick Cole	**1**
The Foamy Brine	BD Feil	
Chasing the Blues Away	Rachel Olivier	
City Music	Rachel Olivier	
White Noise	Nyla Alisia	
Your Sexiest Body Part	Nyla Alisia	
Cold dogs in the back yard	Peycho Kanev	
One Poet in Chicago	Peycho Kanev	
Inexplicable	Peycho Kanev	
Blue impossibility	Peycho Kanev	
About the crisis	Peycho Kanev	

the poem i wrote when i woke up is the same as this one	Adam Wangler	**12**
Layover	George Bishop	
OFF 95	George Bishop	
Razzmatazz	Mike Berger	
Her Scent	Mike Berger	
Muscle Memory	Matthew Brown	

Sonnet to Quaker Meeting in Spring	Roheeni Saxena	
The Catch	Roheeni Saxena	
Holy War	Stiaan Uys	
Soar	Stiaan Uys	
Dirge	Stiaan Uys	
Lonely Sailor	Blanca Blanco	**24**

Unload	Katherine D. Perry	
What it Was Like	Michael Young	
Bless the Scavengers	Michael Young	
Surfacing	Michael Young	
Me and My Son at the Abyss	Michael Young	
Arson	Debrenee Adkisson	
Another Tank	Ted Jean	
Mountain Echoes	Dipika Mukherjee	
Sound Shore in May	Andrea Alterman	
Indigo Bunting	Andrea Alterman	
Metaphor	Will Elliott	**35**
Symbols for Loss and		
the Intangible	Jason Coates	
Void	Jason Coates	
Virgin	Anthony Frame	
Earthling	William Aarnes	
Cicadas	Chelsea Henderson	
Escape	Jill McCabe Johnson	
Fallen Angels	Kevin Del Principe	
Screaming with Silence	J'annine Jobling	
Blind Faith	William Hurst	**47**
Night Vision	Joseph Murphy	
Romance Ends on		
Wedding Day	Alicia Prickett	
Hammer and Anvil	Jon Chan	
A dream of Kansas	Bryan Brunton	
Confessional Poem	Alec Hershman	
Postscript	Alec Hershman	
Provisions	Alec Hershman	
While Picking Out Oranges	Anna Fitting	
Wife says stop cutting trees	Ted Jean	
Oil Spill	Elle Pryor	

one night & a beam of
    light & the city
    of earth   Ben Richardson   **59**
For Sevier Park and the
    Loneliness of Dawn   Ben Richardson
Untitled (Lake Guntersville)   Ben Richardson
The Angel's Silent Fear   Heather Anastasiu
Jo in Wyoming   Linwood Rumney
The River   Linwood Rumney

sonnet to john berryman
    (1914 - 1972)   Adam Wangler
In Weeks Following   Kevin Phoenix
Matches   Nicole Weinberg
Puppeteer   Ian Gammie
Wonder and Madness   Robert Graves

In a Drop of Rain on
    a Spider's Web   Robert Graves   **73**
Writer's Life   Heather LeNoir

The Shadows

The shadows have returned
And have not been thanked
Anchoring down summer's days
Freeing us again to float,

To invent ether, to spill it,
And yet, as if only inverse,
The shadows – especially those
Of trees – are stepped on.

So many things we miss
When gone, though we don't
Know it, we human mesh-
Machines, brains plied
By myriad foreign ships.

How do we choose what to love?

The shadows hit the street
Unwelcomed, again, giving
Substance to light-weight, hefty
Time. But look into a deep pool
Of shade,

Where unnumbered other summers stare.

Patrick Cole

The Foamy Brine

Lately I've been leaving the gate unlatched
and though it moans and wails
like straining boards below deck
or mast bending with sail
it's behind me and out of sight
from the backporch where I watch
out over the cornfield
toward the thin horizon

if I could just sit and wait
for the day to gather
around me like the wild and patient sea
rather than tack into the wind after prizes
chase treasures
hunt what I claim is rightfully mine
but which the day has no intention of letting go
all this I tell myself as I watch into dusk

the gate groans and the corn stirs
slightly at first but then the swell
the wave the inevitable beckoning
I could draw myself up on these sea legs
go round front and simply drop a hook
into an eye and be done with it
but then all this foamy brine
would go draining away
like perfumed suds from a tub

BD Feil

Chasing the Blues Away

Dark
and bitter enough to almost be sweet,
playing tricks on the mind again.
Music and laughter.
Harsh and dirty.
Each to each.
Sad enough to dig across
heart strings and
watch you smile.
Like Magic
in a beat of silence
to make you fall in love
with the stranger
across the room or
the table.

Rachel Olivier

City Music

Notes flute out through the air
as I strum wrought iron fences.
Smiling.
Listening to their true notes.

Changing tones –
a harp resonating –
longer bars bassing out deep,
short bars singing higher.

Beauty rings true.
Birds struggle to sing,
choking in the city air.
But I can still vibrate a chord.

A bar on a city fence rings true.

Rachel Olivier

White Noise

Sometimes the air is quiet,
unmoving.
If I am lucky,
if I stand very still,
the day will pass
right through me.
Other days, most days,
are filled with white noise,
it screams inside me
at a frequency so high,
it takes every atom I have
to hold myself together.

Nyla Alisia

Your Sexiest Body Part

Anyone can turn on your body,
but, what I really want
is to give a hard-on
to your brain.
I want to stimulate your mind,
engage you in the seductive
foreplay of new ideas,
to tantalize your thoughts.
I want to give you
multiple climactic conversations,
leave you reeling,
intelligence exhausted,
mental curiosity spent.
I want to see you
intellectually sprawled out
in the afterglow
of knowledge fulfillment.
Now that would be damned sexy.

Nyla Alisia

Cold dogs in the back yard

There it was – in my pocket!
Oh, what a dangerous traveler I was – with a ticket!
Leaving my country for chasing a dream...
In my other pocket - what was left of my happiness
and luck. I was running away from the black dogs
of sorrow. I thought they can't swim across the ocean.
I was wrong, of course.
And here I am, now. Sitting under the naked light bulb,
sipping the table wine, thinking "Is there a God?"
No answer at all!
I hear the barking of my neighbor's dog. It is dark outside.
In some distant mountain I can feel the snow, I can hear
the wolves run in silence. And now all is so quiet!
The faucet in the kitchen is dripping, the pipes gurgle
and in my lap is this small, old poetry book. I search
for God in there. Nothing! Not even some divinity
of the Word. I continue my search. Outside gets darker than
black. The dog howls. I look up at the light and the brightness
burns my eyes, my wings start to flap. And all of a sudden
I hear a voice:
"Be careful! The bright watchers are still there!"

Peycho Kanev

One Poet in Chicago

This city is scary and supreme.
Its shiny lakeshore with the white yachts
and the seagulls and the herons, tilting
quietly upon the marble waves.
The hard blowing wind
licking the rind of the imposing trees.
Those crazy and beautiful people,
walking up and down the streets,
as Searse tower pierce the alabaster sky.
Long time ago, in some small house,
Carl Sandburg was writing his dreams.
Not too far away, Hemingway learned
his way with the shotgun.
This city of butchers, gangsters
and sky drinking poets.
This city of uncertainty
and misunderstood simplicity.
This city of fondness
and knives leading to oblivion.
But it is still early…
One of those days when you wake up with words
in your head transforming into money…
Unallowable poet's dreams…
God did not give His permission to each and every scrivener.
Cup of coffee or the unsolved color of the whiskey-
which absurd the poet will pick and choose?
This city will take care of it!
Back in the days you could see the little Gwendolyn Brooks
skipping rope with the words forming in her head.
Now, the slam joints are full of screaming typesetters.
This is your place under the sun. City of destiny!
Do not leave it…
The stones of the ruined city wall
will never say: Goodbye!

Peycho Kanev

Inexplicable

I am drinking whiskey from a tin can –
this line sounds so much like blues,
but let me tell you the rest.
This tin can is shiny and red, Oh yes,
many years ago my grandfather
for many years kept his pencils inside
and some small notebook in which he
scribbled later at night. Secret notes about
his past, I presume, then just a blink
of a Supernova and he was gone. After that
my uncle stored in it his old German Luger
which he cleaned almost every day. Maybe he
was afraid of loosing his prolonged quarrels
with cancer and immortality, maybe he wanted
to go on his own terms. My uncle was a great
admirer of Ernest Hemingway. He was gone
one summer Sunday morning. And now the can
is mine. I pour whiskey inside and drink it sitting
in the dark. No music, no light. Just me and the old
whiskey. But it has some strange taste. Almost like
rust from an old pistol and fading memories of words
never written. I lift it close to my ear and I can hear
the whizzing of the chilly mistral, that so long ago
licked the skin of my father. I sigh and say to
the Time in my tin can: Please scholar me as you
collar me, because everything fills. Now and then.

Peycho Kanev

Blue impossibility

I prefer not to see the words that I am writing,
so I take a look through the window:
I see a dog walking outside, sniffing at the trees,
pissing in the bushes- white and brown dog,
and this is real enough to believe in it,
but I say:
Oh, brother this is not possible,
because I do not want to look at the words I am
writing right now,
and the words that I am not writing,
but the blue sky laughs,
the wide and grey sky tilts slowly upon my sheet;
this is impossible –
the fog and the brightness in me opens up,
memories of heavy rain or just my fantasies for rain,
the sounds of the approaching storm are crawling towards me:
I close my eyes –
not wanting to see the words that I am writing,
and I open them up again to see through the window
only this dead dog.

Peycho Kanev

About the crisis

It is in all the newspapers, in Dow Jones,
in all the thermometers, into the victims of the loneliness.
(such a tabular forms are not invented yet).
You got the last months only for yourself.
The men of wisdom declare the last days,
but if they look for us they will find only dust.
To love, because there is no other way out, to feel
the words coming out of your mouth –
when we fall down,
just to restore the eternal cycle,
and we except –
all of us –
(what else we could do?):
the struggle.
It is such a hard work to be honest and true,
when the rest of the world is decomposing.
We are not like them,
we do not talk quietly on the Sunday dinner tables,
we do not communicate with passwords over the phone,
that's the others who peer through the peepholes,
growl at the fences, topple down the Stop signs,
scream at our walls, our last sanctuary –
we are not like them and they can't go without
dragging us out of what was left from the ship,
which is sinking.

Peycho Kanev

the poem i wrote when i woke up is the same as this one

the brightest stars
look down
and bleed your eyes
upon me
and the trees
stirred by a dark wind
bids them dance
a somnambulistic refrain
sighing your name
sweetly
softly
as if in love,
weeping through a
loneliness like no other

let all your secrets
for me drown in
your eyes and be hidden
there, not to tell a living soul
until once again, we meet and
your arms take me in

Adam Wangler

LAYOVER

Two balloons dyed in carnival colors
were making the morning light
deceptively full, the way to work
suspicious. The issues waiting
were well grounded, still packed
in the ice of a restless night.

As darkness dissolved
and the radio insisted I trust
its evanescent claims, I began
to sense the humid, other-worldly
air beyond the steamed windows,
the balloons remaining motionless,
quiet as clouds when the wind's
ready to change.

You don't follow them the way you do
some famous, top secret launch
or a comet about to disappear
for another thousand years.
This is rainbow driven, distance
making it appear as if nobody's
on board but the part of you
that walked out on your wife,
the ropes you cut swaying like ribbons
in your bloodshot eyes.

George Bishop

OFF 95
to a stranger

He wanted to tell me about love
and distance, how their pace and path
move like lines on a weather map.
However, it soon became clear
her features were his own—
the way her lips never met
when she was listening, the tone
of her voice when he wanted to be alone.
He undressed and dressed her
in a few moments, this woman
he'd given half a life, at best,
that I tried breathing beauty into,
the amount I believed she allowed.

So there were two women
and two of us who got to know them
traveling through Georgia, flashes
of friendship here and there, a stain
of doubt deepening mile after mile.
One-sided forecasts filled the bus,
predictable and safe.

Until we turned off 95.
The curve of the exit gave silence
the opening it needed to speak freely.
It was time to tell him distance always wins
but instead I wished him luck, shook his hand.
Changing buses I thought of my own affair
with love's twin, her weakness for what I wanted,
how she still knows I'd die for her.
This far away. This close.

George Bishop

Razzmatazz

The honky tonk piano was playing it hot.
The moonshine was raw not the best of
the lot.

Introducing myself to a table of ladies,
I told them, "I'm big Al, no doubt you've
heard of me." A bevy of giggles followed.
They all laughed but the lady in black.
She looked down her nose and her eyes
said, "Oh please."

Sitting at their table, I bought them a
round drinks. They all seemed pleased
except for the lady in black, who replied,
"Thank you, but I'm good." A pug nosed
blond ranher hand over mine. She batted
her eyes. The lady in black laughed, shook
her head, and looked away

Fascinated, I ask the lady in black to
dance. Taken totally by surprise when
she nodded yes. Her slender body moved
as if it were choreographed. "You're not
like the others," I commented. She
puckered her lips and knitted her forehead
and replied, "I'm not much into juvenile
mating rituals." She paused and stared
into my eyes. "I would appreciate it if
you don't give me your razzmatazz."

All of my favorite pickup lines took to
wing. "I like that," I told her. I stared
deeply into her dark eyes. Her body
and look immediately softened. "You're
the first guy in months I've met that I
don't intimidate." She smiled as she
reply. "Why should I be afraid of a

beautiful woman," I countered.

The music changed, the Ragtime
vanished replaced by soft melodies.
The piano picker must have seen us
in changed from hot to cool. I took her
boldly in my arms and touched my cheek
on hers. Her perfume scent chills down
my spine.

Mike Berger

Her Scent

Not a gorgeous woman, but no plain
Jane. Her eyes are small and she doesn't
have a big lower lip. There is no shine
to her brown hair and no deep dimples.
Her two front teeth are too big and her
skin has a blemish or two. She certainly
doesn't flaunt silicone boobs.

She lights my fire. Her voice is smooth as
the mist that hugs the ocean shore. It's
deep and rich and she always hums a
soft melody. She's also a bright and has
a quick wit. Try to play one ups and you'll
get trashed. For all of that she isn't brassy.

The thing that drives me wild is her scent.
It's much more than her opium perfume. It's
impossible to describe. It isn't a fresh smell
like a summer breeze. It isn't the penetrating
order of a musk ox in heat. It's subtle and
intoxicating. I asked her about it, and she
laughed and told me it was just her hairspray

Mike Berger

16

muscle memory

who doesn't prefer
the chucking of an adze
the slushing of a fore plane
to the squealing of a circular saw
the woodchipper scream of a power plane

what is an hour saved
on a boat to last a lifetime
haste makes it easy to forget
that the body knows the building
better than it knows the thing built

Matthew Brown

Sonnet to Quaker Meeting in Spring

We like to sit in silence gathered here
Within this house of white and birch wood beams
Of after three o'clock sunglow that lie
Across our laps and show us each the light.

We like to sit in silence gathered here
So that we can hear the God's soft whispers
Move gently through our flesh till we're aglow
With sparkling from our own inner light.

We like to sit in silence gathered here
Because the silence makes it easier
For us to hear the dead as they call soft
Over the landscape of the golden hills.

We like to sit in silence gathered here
The silence reminds us to feel the spring.

Roheeni Saxena

The Catch

As flowers are drawn to light, am I drawn,
like charcoal and ash, towards the sea.
It pulls me in and then waits for the shore to
come and claim me, which it never does, because
the ocean is stronger than the fishermen bringing in the catch.

They bring it in under the heat of the sun,
turning themselves brown, burnt, and radiating,
so that the flowers will want to grow towards them.

Roheeni Saxena

Holy War

Silent sandstorm sweeps up screams
Brings blind booming death
A peculiar itch in the eye
Blood-belching guttural gutters
Men's speech slurred a bloody blurb
Holy lungs punctured holily
They speak in tongues.
Divinity resides here
Rapists attend communion
Feast hungrily on body and spirit
Prostitutes thank god in sighing prayer
Each night
The land is holy
Peons move to murder
Whose god is more peaceful?
Shoot the fathers
So the children can praise god
Amongst charred and swollen bodies.

Stiaan Uys

Soar

Her father's wish:
She dives into the broad blue sky
Glides on the wind in harmony
Until she reaches her destination
Builds her nest
Perched on a church's window sill
Gazing down at the world.

Her mother's hope:
She flies majestically
Unfolds her wings with a woman's grace
Loves her offspring
More than she was loved
And raises them to be great
Like her proud mother.

Broken wings were spread
With gray feathers roughed and filthy
And the bird dived
Out the window of a cheap apartment
On the nicotine-stained ninth floor
And soared freely
For four long seconds
Before it crashed into the street
Like dreams and expectations.

Stiaan Uys

Dirge

Another love-child
Of the modern world
Trampled on endlessly,
Warm winds tugged at her
And the earth moved beneath her in unrest,
Trees were torched to light her way
And burned a lingering black
On the horizon, and scorched
Her eyesight like the coffee stains
On the sides of her waitress' apron.
She tried to blink them away,
But the stains stayed until
She frantically slammed shut her eyelids,
Shut out the light,
Created her own and inhaled
The smoke of a different ember
That was killing fashionably,
Yet killing all the same.

That morning the sun rose an hour late
From his disturbed slumber,
And baked the world in sleep-deprived fury -
The hourglass burst from the sun's scolding,
Leaving her to strut over
The sand dunes of time,
With feet shrivelled and blistered and burnt
By the glimmering grains
That already roughed through
Her designer sandals, which now lay
Discarded on a heaped trash pile
That already steeped forty feet high.

But she did notice,
Nor would she care;
She was another love-child
Of the twenty-first century,
Walking on broken promises,
To her thousandth revolution,
To try change the world
For the first time.

The shunned stars shone brightest that night,
When the sun finally found rest
After drinking acid from green clouds.
It was then that the stars drowned themselves
In their own mournful tears and shone no more
For an audience captivated by unnatural light
In an unnatural dark.

But she did not notice,
Nor would she care.

Stiaan Uys

Lonely Sailor

it has come down to this
the feeling of despair causes emotional turbulence
he turns around looks toward the sky
darkness prevails the sound of crickets emanate
as he sits on the curb of the sidewalk
Reminiscing
he can only begin to wonder
about her once

the breeze caresses upon his face
as the air touches upon his lips
he remembers that minty flavor
her morning lips
it only causes a flood of memories
as they caressed his own
the final goodbye

words crossed without significance
feelings rapidly changed
Bitterness
love transforms into rage

Sirens wail like a newborn waking
his responsiveness returns
he rises with a new sense of direction
raring to go

Blanca Blanco

Unload

the dishwasher,
and every plate is
a metaphor: I remember
which sink in which town
gave me that chip or crack;
the tiny glass cup from my great aunt
given before she died when she was
cleaning out her cabinets, a perfect
size for dipping sauces;
pasta bowls from your sister
that are the perfect shape
for black beans with cheese;
forks we stood in the aisles
and compared with every other
box set. We never use the silver
from our wedding gifts.

I admire the cups that have
made all fourteen of our moves
with us, the ones we used in college
before we were too snooty
for Tupperware and all things plastic,
and I stack those right beside
the new metal bottles that make us
somehow feel earth-friendly.

When I put away the cake pan,
the one I found for your birthday
cake, I place it more gently
than needed for a metal frame.
It has held, after all, the silly sugar metaphors
of one person's attempt
to please another.

Katherine D. Perry   --For Charles

What it Was Like

There was a moment I think I meant something else,
when the epiphanies came without hesitations and
second guesses, without the slowing effects of rain
and snow, their deepening doubletalk or precipitous white,
when I walked at a pace in tune not only with light,
the red flash through autumn leaves and those
incalculable jittery descents, but with cabs swerving
off Broadway, with a subway's halts and jumps
through dark tunnels, a discarded bag jolted upward
on invisible pressures, water fanned from fire hydrants,
those stubby symbols of a belief that something can be saved.
Time was there were other ways of becoming, when
generosity meant thankfulness even in desolate times,
even in the dry, gold weed hanging from cracks,
deepening autumn toward winter in the cold gray stone,
or through the streetlight reflected in a puddle
down a narrow alley, that single point of illumination
enriching the dark, the way I stared into the dread,
seized it as a thought and became whole.

Michael Young

Bless the Scavengers

At the horizon, the November sun harvests a crop
of yesterdays, and pierces my bus ride with light
all the way to the Square, at every intersection,
a flash of emblazoned silhouettes, a clock tower,
telephone wires beaded with fiery birds,
mist dampening skyscrapers at the harbor edge,
their sterling window glass kindled in the cold salt air,
vague and burning like a promise, a palimpsest on which
the day is about the be written, shimmering with conflicts
of revision, the possibilities of misdirected traffic,
delayed trains, flooded tunnels or bomb threats.
Although the avenues along this page are not yet
indelible, as long as the mist clings to the streets,
as long as the perspective's scoured by dry leaves,
autumn trees wag their limbs and gulls strafe
wrenching morsels of decay from gutters
and rooftop tiles, like scavenging angels,
clearing the way for a season of second chances.

Michael Young

Surfacing

It's a day when one can hear the morning glories growing,
inching in their curls through the fences,
a kind of rip and snap.

Things buried leach to the surface:
the scratch and shuffle of a woodchuck
tunneling beneath our yard
simmers up through the autumn leaves,
and crickets crawl out from under basement trashcans.

Bone fragments at Ground Zero
are hauled into the afternoon light.
Their marrows cored by five years of decay,
these nuggets of the past,
sifted out of the quotidian,
still glitter with the weight of the day they were buried,
a metal precious enough to transfix any observer.

Unanswered questions return
with the regularity of the photographer's golden time,
the persistence of shadow
lengthening toward the ideal moment,
which is so hard to believe in
though the papers report the next day
how a man on a beach
discovered a bag of unopened letters in the water,
and all of them were prayers addressed to God.

Michael Young

Me and My Son at the Abyss

Even the youngest grasps that our booms and jetties
can't stop its violence, the riptides,
the cross currents and hissing breakers.

To feel its force surging below the surface, life
rising or diving, torn and swallowed and flailing, to sense
the thrust, push and wake of dirt, bits of bone,

kelp, toothed jaws flowering with anemone,
is to know all is equal in this aqueous flux.
Its births consume. It takes the darkest kind of courage

just to dip your toes into it, even touch
its minor whirlpools, let its sand sweep out
from under your heels and feel the constant

sinking. But the primal thrill takes over, and he points
out to the fields where the practiced and foolish
blink between the peaks and says, I want to swim.

He's just now learning
that the clock only goes in one direction, that even mama
and dada can't touch the fire on the stove,

that everyone has limits. I grip his hand
as waves crash around his knees
and he drops, rolling and splashing in the turbulence.

I tighten my hold against the drag tugging him,
pulling him out and down into the power
of its relentless and indifferent honesty.

Michael Young

Arson

He set fire to this temple long ago,
brought his can of lighter-fluid
and doused the place, pouring
extra on the artifacts most golden.

I cried as life went up in flames,
as stars grew pale outside against
the rising cloud of smoke.
The moon dimmed, eaten
by the fire.

I got out and ran, scanned
the night sky for direction, left
a million miles of sand and grass
between us. He stayed put.

I built myself a new house, covered
it in stone and mud and called it
home. It was stronger
than the temple made of gold,
which melts. I had learned a thing or two.

But he came then with his fire can, found
me crouching in a crevice of the
cool house of stone. He flicked the
match and watched it lick up rocky walls.

There was nothing more to melt,
all my treasures were destroyed. I was
not afraid of fire now, and sang a chant
at him from inside blackened walls,
still strong.

Debrenee Adkisson

Another Tank

When gas got real high, I wondered why
I drove around so much, in my ordinary truck,
to Tillamook out to the lighthouse at Cape Meares,
all around Mollala for white gravy and black coffee,
or up the Callapooia to its wraithy falls,
where I rested my head on the wheel a while.

Certainly there is solace in movement;
a Ford F150 is innocent of intrigue; and
the world around here is persuasive of purpose,
even if personal events argue otherwise.

So, four dollars a gallon for regular,
when a gallon gets you eighteen miles
of the Waldo Hills in a glory of swale swollen
with ash and hazel and pond flash, is still a bargain.

Ted Jean

Mountain Echoes

In Bhutan, the mountains call with peals
of prayer bells, mantras churned by brooks
as pilgrims trek a weary path
to the Taktsang Dzong, where a holy man
soared to heavenly heights
on the back of his woman tiger.
Legends spring from rocks here,
of the eternal through ambrosial waters
The Buddha looms large in bhumisparshamudra,
touching earth, rooted here.

Yellow tsatsas, in the red shade of spinning wheels,
mingle cremated ashes into dusty clay,
flags flutter a rainbow salvation,
as two little girls, like kittens in the sun
settle next to me, on the wide rock,
the older speaks haltingly, the younger not at all
yet we play scissors-paper-stone
they teach me Dzongkha, gymtse-dho-shoko
grabbing hands to cut, cover and swallow whole;
it's a language of flashing fingers,
palms turning black-and-white, nap-ya-karp
human babble jostling in amity.

I want them to win.
To always reach out
with such grace, such openness,
to gesture of crows-spider-horses,
to encapsulate a living world
in such mellifluous hands
within tiny folded palms.

Their laughter peals like the prayer bell
over these sheer cliffs, kissed by moist clouds
drenched in holy waters.

Dipika Mukherjee

Sound Shore in May

When we go walking down to that muddy shore
with hiking boots on our feet and binoculars
around our necks we know what we are looking
for, killdeer that will draw us out with their broken
wings until we come too close, sanderlings playing
footsies with the breaking waves as they stand as long
as they can and then flee towards the seaweed scraps
lying above the high tide line. We will turn our backs
to the breeze, let it drizzle us in the smell of salt soaked
mud while we listen to seagulls drop mussels and try
to snatch the cracked remains away from kelp ringed
rocks before another tide or gull gets there first, like
hungry nestlings who cannot stop opening their beaks
in search of morsels from their parents, our eyes look
for more terns, more egrets, and another path to follow.

Andrea Alterman

Indigo Bunting

Feathers the color of your eyes,
quick to fly, hard to follow unless
caught in sunlight, or the odd shadow
play of leaf on top of leaf with a ray
that can't be stopped, a small piece
of sky threw itself into this afternoon's
breeze, and sang for me like you used
to every evening before we drew
your curtains closed on moonless
nights, as if we thought to keep you
closer to us than sky, but you knew
you had to leave our wisp of space,
go back to feathers and flight, touch
mists of curls streaming over rivers,
like the swallows you couldn't stop
for long, like the bunting you had
to catch your feathers in that breeze,
spread your heart past your ribs,
open your beak and sing to your
daydream sky, that bluest eye.

Andrea Alterman

Metaphor

The song says a girl stole your soul.
Well, I can imagine;
She locks the door behind her,
Pulls the curtains shut,
Now everything is grey,
But she is still beautiful.
She sits down on the shag carpet
And shoves her arm
elbow deep into a backpack,
Bites her lip as her fingers grope
(they are bitten fingernails)
Inside the crowded darkness
Her eyes widen—there it is
Past the compact and nestled
Beneath the faded paisley wallet,
Swaddled in fast food napkins,
A smallish box
She reclaims her arm, lip licking,
And lets the shadows drip from her wrist
Her hand bathed now in the secluded dim
Of this secret place
The box is somewhat heavy in her palm,
And she smiles strangely,
And opens…

A glamouring soul
So small a thing
Yet so luminous and bright
That her pupils shrink in the stolen glow.

Will Elliott

Symbols for Loss and the Intangible

What is this necessity for meaning?
Like the rose
that sits awkwardly angled
on my arm—is it not
but ink contained within a boundary,
pressed into a larger surface of skin?
How I feel about it now
compared to the day of its conception,
when I sat as a boy dreaming
about women as the needles turned me
numb, does not change its colors
or shadows—or its fading
or the reality of a world dimming
because we each have a different relationship
with the sun. I once told a man

when discussing the meaning of things
that I wished I could be a bear— he asked,
"Why didn't you get that tattooed on your arm?"
"There is still a chance I will become
a bear, and for a bear to have a tattoo
of a bear seems silly," I replied.

Jason Coates

Void

There is something necessary
about the sensation of opening
a door and brushing against
the shoulder of a stranger slightly turned
inward and the breeze that is born
as the outside world is invited through
the threshold fractions at a time.
Fractions of time dissolve the thin walls
of metal and glass and bolts
washers rubber hinges springs knobs
locks: the constructions of men
who regulate the conditions of a world
they impose themselves upon.
In a space situated as the equilibrium
of suction and thrust,
the climate sustains—no wind,
no rain, no dream of a flood;
there are only the missing parts of things
touched and craved but never known
and perhaps never believed.

Jason Coates

Virgin

I've never been here before,
standing at Holly's apartment
for the fourth time this week,
the peep hole staring at me
indignantly. I want to look
through it, see our world small,
before she opens the door,
her smile half-cocked so sarcasm
can prevent sentimentality,
awkward small talk about football
or our students' latest papers.
We're both thinking about sex.
I feel, for the first time ever, small,
aware of my body, my bones,
the thin hairs under my armpits.
Aware that the windows are naked.

* * *

I've been naked before
summer camp bathrooms
walking aimlessly through my apartment
group showers after track practice at my Catholic high school

and once when I was seven
I took the garbage out naked
just to see if alarms would go off
announcing my skin and nuclear war
if the police would come
breaking down the doors
shooting me with cameras
if I would feel ashamed or scared
surrounded by paper plates
surrounded by bags of pop cans
surrounded by air

but I was just naked
and the neighbor's dogs barked
unamused
and the television in the basement
was loud enough to drown out my shivers

* * *

You know I played Jesus' body
in my junior high school's Passion Play.
And I told you how I only wore shorts.
But hung on the cross, I thought about sex.
I was fourteen, so it wasn't the first time.
I figured Jesus was a virgin,
a stoic man, but mostly because
he was so busy healing lepers,
making wine, dying for our sins, rising
from the dead. But I bet he was attractive,
his arms hardened by carpentry, his skin
olive and sun-stained, that deep male voice
that had to have tempted the Galileans,
and his shoulder blades sticking out like
residual wings. I didn't want to think
about Jesus and sex and the cross,
my brand new chest hairs exposed to the crowd,
my rib cage pushing against my thin skin,
my legs defined by my visible fibulas.
I was fourteen and afraid of playing dead,
being carried away on a fake cross,
with God staring at my erection.
I was now a man of the world
desperate for a flag to call my own.

* * *

And the virgin mother
told her fiancé that
she was with child. She soothed
herself by rubbing
her belly, still small

but full of divine
cellular division.
She watched her fiancé
pace, dust on the floor
rising with each sandal-step,
his stomach heavy with age
but his hands still callused,
his chipped fingernails
housing dirt and his eyes
soft despite his angry brow.
And her fiancé slammed
his fist on a table,
demanded the truth,
spit flying from each
ancient and cursed syllable.
He studied her face,
the white dot on her pupils,
the wind-ripped lumps lining
her cheeks, the subtle tilt
of her eyebrows that would
forever turn him on,
as he settled for an embrace,
each hand studying
each holy body.

* * *

I used to punch my penis,
like a dance, a ritual
call for rain to shower the sins of man
upon all men. God and sex and
I'm forever nailed to a fake cross,
knowing the sudden shock to my groin
won't feel better with the next punch.
Ginsberg might have been pornographic,
and Dickinson thought Whitman was obscene,
so what am I
with my thoughts of Holly,
my Eve in the garden,
the smell of her feet

pungent with mud and moss,
her breasts brushing against ash leaves,
my blind fingers
sliding across her hips and down her legs,
my beard tickling her belly,
her pink ankles,
and I want to remind her
that I've never done this before,
that I still think
she's the mother of God,
that when we die
we go to heaven naked.
Who'll need wings then?

Anthony Frame

Earthling

The airport walkway
moves you along,
your lope having slowed
to a standstill,
your bag drawn close behind you,
ahead of you
the hurried two-hour drive
to your sister's bedside

and you're thinking
that at 195
you're 20 pounds heavier
than the largest wolf
ever shot,

a thought
the book tucked
in a pocket of your bag
has led you to savor

though you're 62
and less a hunter
than any wolf you've outlived
and too weary
and too guarded
to lift your head
in these surroundings
and wail.

William Aarnes

Cicadas

It darkens. The sun drowns in the horizon
and never resurfaces, leaving us to our hands
and lips beneath a charcoaled sketch of sky.
Azaleas in white for the occasion,
wine humming in our glasses whenever the wind
casts a careless hand. For the versions of each other
we can't understand, we offer small mercies—
a moon in full bloom, the hollows
of your cheekbones pooled in darkness,
bread crumbs littered in the grass like dew.
Lilac, you say, when the rain begins,
my hair washed in the scent of it. Cicadas,
I tell you, while they drone in the trees,
remembering a wreath I once saw wound
with their brittle skins, their bodies emptied
at last of longing. Somewhere a pair
of sleepless hands meets piano keys, strains
of Debussy ribboning out the open window.
No one makes any promises. April edges quietly
back the way it came, petal and skin and thirst
in its wake, ear pressed to its own vanishing.

Chelsea Henderson

Escape

I should have been a jeweler.
Six months on the coast
selling trinkets to tourists,
six months on another coast
making snake bracelets
in some shanty town where the mind
can follow a trash-lined but glittering
footpath to the beach.

I should have been a fly-fisherman.
Kick off my shoes,
let the earth uncoil
a perfect arcing cry
from my soles through my arm whipping
to the hook end of a hickory pole,
glazed fish bedazzled and slicing
open the incredulous water and sky.

I should have been a priest.
Holiness scattered with a flick
of the fingers, a blessed mist
broadcast to masses fidgeting
guiltily in their pews, waiting
to receive the dangerous sacraments
of communion, confession,
deliverance and grace.

Jill McCabe Johnson

Fallen Angels

Ugly organ crows
Move to pierce your soul
Their lazy light shines
Through desperate storms

We're in the garden child
Whisper to me
Everything's going to be alright
This night is only the night

If you want a piece of me
Take them all
They're all your
Lonesome lullabies bright eyes

Irascible dreams walk
Miles across my skull
Until they settle
Like small fallen angels

Kevin Del Principe

Screaming with Silence

A flock of words, battering.
So much to be screamed!
Despair
Gags her mouth, and
The hurt birds tumble behind her eyes.

A walk in the woods and the frail green leaves.
A green pond. Algae feeds
On her reflection.

A desert lies behind her eyes.
In this vast and burning place
The shot birds shriek.

J'annine Jobling

Blind Faith

Tiresias taps
his cane, a prophet
singing his way
into old Jerusalem.

Blues ooze from
the gash of his mouth;
he can't wade out
into the swirling pool.
He's devout
as far as
he can feel
with a three
foot pole and legions
of eyes nailing
him to the soiled tile wall of the
subway.

William Hurst

Night Vision

Riding night's
Sea-born breeze

Our one moon seemed ageless

Trailing stars
Across the tide
Scented ash
And circled stones

As we woke
From childhood

Oars in hand
Hearts pitching
Keels well-honed
By desire
And hope

Prows linked

Sails
The width of breakers
The breadth
Of foam

Joseph Murphy

Romance Ends on Wedding Day

Romance ends on wedding day:
The movies show it. Chase,
Catch, kiss, cut, credits.

Ignore that unpleasant side-effect (marriage).
There. Learn to love to tug the leash, "Let me at 'em,"
And live never to catch. The catch kills the hunt.

This swooning, dating, waiting, flying,
Quickly-dying fire burns a generation out
On second-degree romance. The quiet promise proves

Less exciting than the obstacle and the lure.
Alone, each fighter fortifies her question
Against its wandering, unwanted answer—

That love is hard. Relationships throb and pus like wounds.
The jagged edged of two souls wound each other,
While aphids and mildew squat on rosy lover's lane.

Our infatuations pick a fight, then (cowards) back away,
Never linking arms to wrestle through
The throbbing, rending, pestilent mildew

To find the wedding aisle is not the destination,
But the first thirty feet of a red-flagged hike
Too dangerous, too steep and cragged to take alone.

Alicia Prickett

Hammer and Anvil

Upon the anvil the steel sits.
And there it meets the anvil
A strike is made, sparks fly
The steel bends but does not break
With molten fire the steel regains its shape
For a curl to straight
The hammer sings again, sailing through the air.
So it strikes again, in a different place
The steel buckles, it sweats red-gold sweat
Its agony rings through the anvil
But the anvil is deaf
The hammer retreats to gain higher ground
From there it lets physics to bring it to sally forth
And so it comes
For the steel, who cannot survive another
The steel flips onto its edge, ready to receive.
A raw razor's furry, untested yet full of vigor
And so the hammer shatters.
The anvil is driven from the field.
As the day goes the steel cools.
The heat that held it together dissipates
It crumbles, thrown back into the furnace to be reformed.

Jon Chan

A dream of Kansas

Down a narrow stretch of road that divides the cornfields
between Holton and Topeka Kansas, I am on my Big Wheel,
a yellow and red plastic tricycle.

Between my legs the oversized black wheel spins
so well on the summer-hot asphalt that I am concerned only
with leaning back and breathing in the sun and
the flashing-green expanse rising to either side of the road.

There is a smell of asphalt which is overcome by a thicker
cornfield odor of life. The rows of tall stalks hold up
the tangled silks of overflowing ears of corn.

Everything seems to be in place.
I have one crooked leg for the field on the left
and one crooked leg for the field on the right,
and one hand on each end of the handlebar
from which long strips of golden plastic stream back
on either side of the tricycle,
snapping back up in the hard wind
small grains of sound and light.

A motorcycle appears from behind on its way to Topeka.
We race for a time before I motion that the Big Wheel
has had enough, and the motorcycle disappears
over a hill on the road ahead.

Moments later I am awake,
stand from bed in an early morning light
and breathe two words – thank you.

Bryan Brunton

Confessional Poem

And when the hummingbird of sleep
Refuses to come into focus, this paper seems
The only way to recuperate- whispers whitely
For human secrets, human sequences, so:

A human can slump into sloth,
Slumber without substance,
Or instead depend eventually upon nothing
But the ground to hold its weight,
Or, equally shifting, the beacon faces
Of help and reason -not quite the field,
But somewhat the fireflies there.

A human can bang its head
On the steering column of sleep in gridlock,
Can go, in fact, a dozen or more of what once
Were called days and meant something
Without allowing the mind, spinning
Infinite in its maple seeds to make way

For dreaming. A human can squeeze too hard
What may have held at one time, attraction, lose its mystic glue-
That which comes to be called 'attraction', or
"The ease before knowing", or finally just "lost"-
Can simultaneously spend a lifetime of sleepless moments
Trying to get it back;
When nostalgia becomes its own
Harness, mode, harshness,
An unparseable when.

But when it wants to be discreet,
What I really want to know is
Can I say so and recover?
If I've left the good parts out-
Said not enough
When I promised too much

-If I just went to bed,
Would you hold it against me?

Alec Hershman

Postscript

The telephones still run their relay, yes.
A squirrel-bandit with a blue rubber-band
Slinks across the tightrope, node to node.

In the old theater they used to throw apples of invective,
Boo-lobs of tomato. "Aw shucks,"
Says my companion of the curb-side circus,
And chucks a nut.

There is a difference in dust, my love
Between kicking it and kicking it up;
First the rye-residue of the morning turned afternoon;
Later the few missing things I return to.

In our repertoire no good words
For boredom. The petty disappointments
Until courtesy became a pair of handcuffs.
We never wanted easy. Discarded garments always
Made a sandbar, slowing down the dream-room.

These mornings I wake to
Too dumb to get the joke.
Signals, perhaps, the cow-lick transistors
The serifs of smoke.

I dawdle in the broken hull
With last week's papers, crowding
Last week' coffee rings. The Parade of Stasis—
Yes—the white noise in every printed thing.

Alec Hershman

Provisions

Because I have not wed I don't know how
My husband's mother grows so patient—
Wears the blanket, first on one, then the other

Shoulder. We sit and smoke and count
Our blessings. In my palm—a mineral impulse
Even as a rumor of snakes could draw us

Breathless at a finger's whispering.
Sentences begin with "Have I really....."
And end no better for it. When I braid her hair

She shrugs, unto others, and doesn't blame me
And there remains some tenderness although
We do not name it or its brief illuminations.

Alec Hershman

While Picking Out Oranges

I lingered easy, July-sweltering
beside the fruit stall in the market street.
Shoveling my hands through the oranges
for the heaviest most medium-firm.
Across from me, diligent, stood
the fishmonger and his slender pairing knife
a living bullfrog
worming to slip against the choke
of the man's brine sopping
yellowed dish gloves. .
He pressed that knife, glinting,
clear against the neck of the frog,
its back legs still paddling, treading air
and sliced across the palpitating bulge of the throat
pushed four fingers into the neat slit,
tugged back and clean-stripped away the skin
like the frog had been thrown together
from sun warped rubber
and too little glue.
The kicking was over,
And the thing just hung there;
joints and sinews
shining naked flesh,
pinkish, the color of little girls' cheeks
limp in the man's fist.

Anna Fitting

Wife says stop cutting trees

Big leaf maple is just a weed, after all,
despite its burly limbs and leafy tuck,
its seed hordes sifting on spiral wings,
suckers exploding by gobs out of burl
to occlude any space that isn't maple.
Now, recognize, simply, that this is raw:
to beat all the others for space and rain;
so that I must cut it, shouting chainsaw,
to its seepy stump, and buck and split it,
to season for firewood an indifferent year,
to burn in our upstairs bedroom fireplace,
a ligneous fireworks for love-making,
and after, to tabulate in drowsiness
the final detonations of a big woody weed.

Ted Jean

Oil Spill

Creosote, brutal brown floating
mess and darkness,
stuck in a whirlpool of
never ending butterfly strokes.
Lumbering through black mud
and circling clumsy arms,
consuming oily glue bubbles,
which destroy the germs of mobility
with insults and scorn.

Living here quietly imprisoned,
everybody else is moving,
breath leaves their lips.
The water, the engines
all sound identically muffled
as tar falls slowly through my body.
Legs clasped by phantom hands,
never swim, can only drift,
spinning away directionless until,

lullaby time, rocked and soothed
gently to the dirty bank
onto waking land.

Elle Pryor

one night & a beam of light & the city of earth

i've called with wild eyes
and wild hours
on flickering drums
flared moon flowers and the street lamps
ballooning like membraneous and orchestrated throats
shot through with spires of quivering dark
that flutter and vanish and flounder into light.

this is where the earth happens
this is where the earth is
shelled into some pocket of
riveting silence echoing an electric hum where
a misplaced plastic-beamed ray
falls as it may as it would have fallen
without me without your heart that beats in
mine in the red clay bricks and the grasping
fingertips of deep-night dew sweating
and forming and holding all in cambered yawing domes
on mailboxes and puddles that cradle cigarette butts
and black hand railings of rolled corrugated iron and
sticky fresh paint on the fence
where the earth happens
where the mosquitoes are sunk
in humidity and anchored by a nameless solemnity
to the slats of wood brushed by bluegrass and zoysia
and long rooted runs of bermuda
coming out of the earth to be
where the earth happens
to catch my wild eyes and haunt the wild hours
and search in all the wrong places for unhatched
glowworms and the what may be of nighttime.

Ben Richardson

For Sevier Park and the Loneliness of Dawn

Old man stretched lean in sunrise shadow,
bent at waist as dusty, furled newspaper,
clearing sticks and pocketing slips of
paper that slowly peel from rain dark roads.
Ten steps up, the wife and little dog, clicking.
Abandonment. . . and after fifty-two years.
(Perhaps I can't understand half-century
long, sprawling, detached love.)
His life necessitates the toil of
clearing roads
-- tree limbs, asphalt, glass, and plastic.
-- hubcaps, beer cans, and cigarette butts.
Cursing storms, painters, and
the garbage truck driver.
Spent his life
clearing roads,
one
after
another.
First, the drive, smothered in snow.
Then, the Fourth of July confetti.
Sticks to rubber soles
in asphalt heat.
Another time -- daughter's wedding
(Best Man sick on patio).
The ice-storm when his mother's great oak
came down in the driveway, catching
Cadillac bumper and taillights.
Yellow plastic like seed heads
in the cracked concrete.
And summer: he took a push-broom to
a sidewalk full of sweetgum balls,
grandson's red tricycle ploughing
fields of chalk mazes and flowers.
Now it's the wife, the dog, and early fog,

and they've left him clearing
rain dark roads in the public park.

Ben Richardson

Untitled (Lake Guntersville)

Now the sky has smeared over in a gray wash, and
Now the trees have all turned blue above the black water,
as if burning in a thin, transient smoke.
Now a fishing line hangs from the sweetgum,
silhouetted against the sky,
carving the lake into perfect halves, and
Now my brother is dredging a pond scum darker than night
with his overweight lure.
Now a wind is clearing away the fog, and
Now the water dances with a thousand roiling circles
as the clouds charge on the morning.
Last night I stumbled out of the darkness of summer
into the blackness of summer,
And the asphalt was sweating out city heat
from its curved back like some primordial sea creature.
From the couch in your backyard, the fence was burning,
and the fence turned to vapors
in the shadows of lambent flames.
I said to you, what should I do with my life?
And you said, is it a girl? And it's always a girl.
And the truth sprang at me like the clasping, severed head
of a moccasin that can't relinquish. Even in death. But,
Now my shirt is soaked, the limbs are sagging, and
my brother hangs a weightless fishing line from his shoulders.

Ben Richardson

The Angel's Silent Fear

In Heaven there are faithful creatures—
glorious angels, each with a hundred eyes,
all of them trying to catch
a glimpse of God,
—though they know to do so
would force God to smite them
down to hell or earth—
so they cover
their eyes with fire-wings
to singe their eyelids
into blind obedience.
Do not linger.
Do not look.

Do not seek what God has given
to man: His image. His breath
—life to dust—
You awe-ful angels are elders but not
sons. Not sons of God
like the mortals you watch
with each of your hundred gleaming eyes,
glaring at their depravity
—millions in a single blink—
and yet still never able
to catch a glimpse of their beauty
before it is mired
in their shit.
Do not linger.
Do not look.

Because your secret terror,
oh ye faithful centurion angel,
is that the God upon whom you may never gaze
is just as ugly, just as putrid
—with the ravenous
consuming and excreting—

as the man made in His image,
that the God who tells you to hide
your eyes from His glory, too
has a precious secret: like man,
he loves the hideous and cruel.
Do not linger.
Do not look.

Heather Anastasiu

Jo in Wyoming

Summertime, 1946.
The prairie grass sunbaked yellow.
From the backseat of a Packard—
silver flash of the dashboard,
wooden panel more richly textured
than any of his landscapes,
Hopper paints his wife Josephine
painting a mountain in Wyoming.

Jo, the only woman who modeled
for him after they married. Jo,
a virgin and an artist when they wed—
the template if not the muse for all
the Hopper women, mostly shown
nude—sagging breasts and
jowls and narrow hips—
as he sketched studies.

In her diaries, she reports
she burnt her leg on the stove
while strutting for The Girlie Show.
In the painting muscles tense
and glisten from the strain of heels
as the angry stripper twirls
a silk shawl—her nipples absurdly
redder than her hair. With Jo posing,

Hopper drafted countless women
crawling in and out of bed.
At the window, the flush cheeks
of Hopper's fantasies mock
our blushes. "It was entirely
for him," she writes of sex,
and left her feeling "subnormal,"
especially "attacks from the rear."

"His lighthouses are all self-portraits,"
she claims. "At Cape Elizabeth,
it was pitiful to see all the poor
dead birds that had run into them
on a dark night." But in Wyoming,
with no harsh angle of sun,
Hopper reveals Jo in all her clothes

and all her pleasure. Hair tied up,

no sudden wind can hide her smile
as she glances at a mountain
too cluttered for Hopper's tastes.
Her husband's jacket tossed
over the seat to remind us who
the driver is, Jo appears neither
lonely nor alone as her brushstrokes
near a summit we cannot see.

Linwood Rumney

The River

On the bank my dog recovers an eel.
He thinks his duty is to place it at
my feet—head torn off, body lacerated
by the dam's turbines. The stench
is horrible—sulfur and brine.
By instinct I fling it back.
My dog retrieves it. Years ago,
Danny and I discovered a nest
of eels in a boulder's eddy
upriver. We fished out all we could,
mutilated them with dull jack knives
and chucked the severed parts into
the river. We fished all morning,
frenzied by the spectacle of writhing
dismembered corpses, until he mistook
a vagrant head for a stone he meant
to launch at a decapitated body
still lurching through ripples.
The gaping jaw clamped hard
onto his ring finger, and Danny,
startled by this will to feed even
after death, gouged his own
knuckle to rip it off.
This headless and persistent
supplicant does not surprise me.
It seeks an audience to ask
after its reluctant groom.

Linwood Rumney

66

sonnet to john berryman (1914 - 1972)

A greater poet, (though no greater than you)
could do little justice to thee, an ant's assent
of a mountain, or a man believing in his heart that
he understands woman is an image of this.

I can see you now, behind glasses and above
a Rasputin beard, (hiding madness not meant
for normal sober speech)
rattling out rigormortis dreams of
mr bones -

Henry and his nameless friend, both faceless as
machines, timid before the gods. There,
there stands death looking over
their shivering shoulders down the long
drop of the bridge.

Adam Wangler

In Weeks Following

If the early petals drain
Into poisoned wrinkled auburn
By the spores and knotted ivy underneath,

And the red and yellows peel
Into decay of damp cinders
Bruised under roots anchored by hard green,

Let me remember
The bloom that surrounds the lilac days.
The white dress suspended by honey
And soft morning glory.

When the needles fall,
May they sew the linens of the earth.
And the eulogies of winter.

That the cloth of powdered april
Lay to catch the tears of may.

kevin phoenix

Matches

four years ago, your girlfriend burned
and you stayed with her until the scars healed

you had scattered candles among the sea of take-out cartons,
and as she leaned outside to exhale
tobacco smoke, she forgot
about that effort

you watched her long skirt spark as her torso hung from the half-
opened window
and your synesthetic mind saw, not blazes enveloping shins,
but the taste of summer peaches;
you wondered if she'd ever gone picking
and you could barely stop yourself from trying to sample
the sunbursts as they lapped at her thighs

now i perch at the edge of your bed,
skin tender, malleable as raw dough
and envious, not of the heat, but the gesture,
draping myself in flammable fabric,
hungry for the occasional ember

Nicole Weinberg

Puppeteer

Be a doll and I'll wave hello
like a sappy young thing
to her inscrutable itness.
Bat my eyes, be predictable.
Make me smile broadly:
show off eight years of braces
and dedicated retainer use;
how faithful I've been, locking my mouth up every night.

She loves my sense of style,
you know,
how inherently interesting it is.

And it goes:
I might, I will, I do, blush, bliss, clash, wave goodbye.

Pull my strings for animation,
play my recorded lines on her answering machine.
Talk of her itness to the man behind the bar,
not too sweet.
If she drops a hint on the telephone,
kidnap it,
ransom it for another and another
until you're satisfied with my fall.

Tap the keys in that familiar pattern:
the gunshot and single tear on her cheek.
Never end with a twist.

When I let the strings sag, bow deeply.

I fell for her when you weren't looking,
I fell for the tones in her laugh.
But you couldn't hear them;
even as you mumbled the exact pitch between pursed molars.

My fingers,
they twitched
on the trigger's cold skin;
I couldn't have pulled it myself.

Ian Gammie

Wonder and Madness

Wander in cascades released
from vice-like, vile virtues.
The spring muses ride the fields;
our sleds strand in the madness of choking weeds.
And crystallized in a window frame,
the pale moon reminds of cold flesh.

We are wandering wombs
and wondering crypts.
We begin and end
in one wheezing breath,
one fit of violent charity.

Yet we hope our fitfully writing,
our microcosms of sentences,
our quantum words,
our theoretical theses,
or perhaps our relative essays can sum
the physicists' numbers
with the Numbers of God,
or at least save us from the next black rat's fleas. . . .

Comb the countless waves,
the countless years:
All cities lie beneath,
their walls surrendered,
their treasures washed clean,
stolen by the dull sword of time.

Robert Graves

In a Drop of Rain on a Spider's Web

With six legs and seven hearts,
with an empty-eyed gaze,
with the faces in the window, looking in,
with the peasants, I am with the peasants,
and the whiteness of our page is thick
and heavy with rain clouds.

The expanding design is woven into splash rings.
The puddles dance in the deluge.
The spider pricks its eight legs across the sticky web,
where spatters of rain cling.
And within a drop of water on a spider's web
there is a door to another world.

I remember looking down into the dark of the old well.
I thought there should be the glint of sun on water
within the dark patterns of brick and mortar, or
maybe a shimmering refection on the circular wall.
I remember the darkness dizzying me down.

And in a drop of rain on a spider's web
there is light and cohesion – surface tension
maintained by the existence of an inner door;
surface tension born of inward expansion.
But looking inside, I condensed.
I fell like rain into the white morning

and into the web – just a six-legged peasant
in the clutches of a predatory master,
just a seven-hearted slave
to the many-eyed breaker –
the vampire, the emptiness
that sews its dark designs in my eyes.

Robert Graves

Writer's Life

Click click click
goes the pen waiting
for the mind to awaken

Tap tap tap
on the barren page

Tick tick tick
goes the unforgiving clock
reminding you the world is
continuing without you.

Heather LeNoir

CPSIA information can be obtained at www.ICGtesting.com
Printed in the USA
LVOW01s1052170913

352813LV00001B/38/P

9 781453 827802